1 | ACCELERATION

UNLOCK YOUR G(
ACCELERATE YOUR JO

THE WIDMAN UNIVERSITY KINGDOM ACCELERATOR COURSE

Learn how to leverage your gifts, market and sell products and services, build momentum, and achieve lasting impact in every area of life.

IT'S TIME FOR YOU TO ACCELERATE!
SCAN THE QR CODE TO JOIN WIDMAN UNIVERSITY!

Go to www.docmurphy.net/events

ACCELERATION

The Season of Maturity and Momentum

Doc Murphy

Doc Murphy Movements
Plano, Texas

Copyright © 2025 by Doc Murphy.

All rights reserved. No part of this book may be
reproduced or transmitted in any form or
by any means, electronic or mechanical, including
photocopying, recording, or by any
information storage and retrieval system, without
permission in writing from the copyright
owner.

Unless otherwise indicated, all Scripture quotations are
taken from the King James Version of the bible.

Some scripture quotations are the author's paraphrase.

This book was printed in the United States of America.

Doc Murphy Movements
2220 Coit Rd. Ste 480-123
Plano, Tx. 75075

ISBN- 9798306470344

Published by Everywhere Publishing

For Booking and to order additional copies of this book, contact:

Doc Murphy Movements
pastordocmurphy@gmail.com
www.docmurphy.net

CONTENTS

0. Introduction………………………….......…..5

1. God is a God of Acceleration…………..6

2. The Liam Paul Acceleration……………11

3. Things are Taking Too Long……………16

4. The Liam Paul Discernment……………23

5. Make IT so You Can Make it……………28

6. The Liam Paul Strategy…………………32

7. The Power of Momentum………………35

8. The Liam Paul Momentum………………40

9. …When You Know This…………………43

10. The Liam Paul Hidden Treasure………49

11. Everything Restored in a Day…………55

12. The Liam Paul Restoration……………62

13. Accelerated Business in a Day…………68

14. The Liam Paul Business Solution……..74

15. Precision, Shifts, and Passive Income..80

16. The Liam Paul Precision…………………86

17. The Liam Paul Mastery…………………90

18. Bonus Chapter……………………………93

ABOUT THE AUTHOR…………..100

Introduction

We are in a season of maturity. This means we are coming into our own. We can handle Kingdom success and experience all God has for us. This is also a season of acceleration where things that have taken a long time are now going to speed up. Those who have humbled themselves by being obedient to God will be exalted in this season (1 Peter 5:6). This is due season. You have served, given, lived the life, sown into others, helped others, loved others, and pursued your purpose with great passion and faith. It's your time to receive. It's your time to experience the harvest. You've planted the seeds, and it's harvest time (Galatians 6:9). Things that took years will now be a matter of days (Amos 9:13). Satan has done everything in his power to hinder or block you, but no longer will he be able to (1 Thess 2:18). Once you discern that it's him, use your authority and resist him. Push him back and kick down every door that he closed. Get ready to accelerate into your mature season! Let's go! - Doc Murphy

Chapter One: God is a God of Acceleration

When needed and in certain seasons, God will help speed things up. It's miraculous and goes against natural laws. Things that would take years can take a day with God. I wrote a song a few years back called *"By This Time Tomorrow,"* inspired by 2 Kings 7:1, where God worked a miracle and shifted the prices so the people could afford what they needed. He supplied their needs and did it speedily.

2 Kings 7:1 Elisha replied, "Listen to this message from the LORD! This is what the LORD says: ***By this time tomorrow in the markets of Samaria, six quarts of choice flour will cost only one piece of silver***, and twelve quarts of barley grain will cost only one piece of silver."

God can make the prices go down. In this scenario, it's not just about making more money but about working with God and taking advantage of the opportunities and miracles He provides during certain seasons. He can help speed up your situation!

Amos 9:13-15 "Yes indeed, it won't be long now." God's Decree. "***Things are going to happen so fast your head will swim***, one thing fast on the heels of the other. You won't be able to keep up. Everything will be happening at once—and everywhere you look, blessings! Blessings like wine pouring off the mountains and hills. I'll make everything right again for my people Israel:

They'll rebuild their ruined cities. They'll plant vineyards and drink good wine. They'll work their gardens and eat fresh vegetables. And I'll plant them, plant them on their own land. They'll never again be uprooted from the land I've given them."

Acceleration means the capacity to gain speed within a short time. It implies advancement and furthering.

Declutter and Organize Your Life and Business

Taking too long to find things creates frustration and a sense of wanting to give up. When things aren't organized, it slows you down. You're spending too much time on unnecessary things.

I've had to organize my life and declutter things. I use the Evernote app to organize my notes, goals, songs, plans, businesses, churches, etc. I put things in categories and folders. It helps save time. I can find things

8 | ACCELERATION

easier and quicker. Disorganization slows things down.

How Do You Ponder Things?

Sometimes your mind is so cluttered with mess, bitterness, fear, worry, too much figuring, analyzing, and trying to learn too much that you end up doing nothing. Declutter your mind and make it focus. You have to be disciplined to do this. You have to find a target and aim only at it. If not, a cluttered mind will not only slow you down but cause you to do nothing at all.

Trying to figure out what you want to do is slowing you down. Trying to figure out what you're supposed to be doing is slowing you down. You need to **do** who you are! Who are you? What are your genuine skills? What are your God-given abilities and purpose in life? You have to put in time to get those priorities in each day—10 minutes, 20 minutes, 30 minutes…get it in. You are taking steps. Get healthy so you can have enough energy to work a job or run a business and do your purpose at the same time. You do this consistently until you can do what you truly desire.

Get Your Life Organized

9 | ACCELERATION

Who should you be friends with right now? Stop trying to be everyone's pal. Whose house should you be visiting? Who are your mentors? Categorize them, focus on their wisdom, and take action. What conferences should you attend (outside of your local church)? What business should you be focused on right now? What books should you be reading? You're not organized—this is one reason things are going so slow.

Get a plan for each day. These will be your daily missions. Go on a 30-day mission. Know what book you will read, who you will meet with, what you will work on for that day, and just focus on one day at a time. Watch how much you accomplish. Don't let distractions hinder you. You have to be disciplined to declutter.

What speeds you up is a decluttered, focused, and prioritized life. What are the essentials? If you want radically different results, then you will have to get radical. This means you need to eliminate things that are distractions: social media, entertainment, foolish and meaningless phone conversations.

I recall a successful businessman saying he didn't deserve entertainment or social media until he became a millionaire. He disciplined himself and did what others wouldn't do, and in record-breaking speed, he reached his goal.

He focused and learned what he needed to learn and put things in place, which positioned him for success. People want miracles, but what they need is maturity. They need to grow up through discipline, self-control, focus, and the elimination of things that are keeping them from reaching their goals.

Chapter Two: The Liam Paul Acceleration

Liam Paul lived in a bustling urban complex called Everywhere Park. The modern-style living complex wasn't just his residence; it was a vibrant hub of innovation and community. Liam wasn't your typical businessman. He didn't just aim for success—he pursued purpose. A devout believer, Liam knew that his calling was more than financial gain; it was about being a catalyst for change.

One morning, as sunlight streamed through the large windows of his minimalist apartment, Liam sat at his sleek glass desk, poring over his notes. His life had felt sluggish lately—business deals delayed, plans postponed, and progress stalled. Frustration gnawed at him, but he knew this was just a season.

That morning, he read from **2 Kings 7:1**: *"By this time tomorrow in the markets of Samaria, six quarts of choice flour will cost only one piece of silver, and twelve quarts of barley grain will cost only one piece of silver."* The words struck him like lightning. He had always believed in the power of God to accelerate progress, but now, it felt personal. By this time tomorrow... Could things really change that fast?

12 | ACCELERATION

Liam leaned back in his chair, pondering the passage. The story of Elisha reminded him that God could shift circumstances in an instant. Prices, opportunities, even entire economies could change when God was involved. The thought was both exhilarating and sobering.

Later that day, Liam decided to take action. He opened his laptop and began organizing his notes using the Evernote app. He had heard about the importance of decluttering and knew he needed to implement it in his life. His files were a mess—business ideas, client contacts, marketing plans—all jumbled together. It took hours, but by evening, he had everything neatly categorized.

With his mind clearer, Liam set a goal: he would go on a 30-day mission to declutter his life and focus on acceleration. Each day, he would tackle one area—whether it was his schedule, his relationships, or his spiritual life. He believed that by eliminating distractions, he would create space for God to move.

The next morning, Liam woke up with renewed energy. He had a meeting with a potential investor who had shown lukewarm interest in his real estate venture months ago. To his surprise, the investor was now eager to partner with him. *"Things are going to happen so fast your head will swim,"* he remembered from

13 | ACCELERATION

Amos 9:13-15. He smiled, recognizing that God was already at work.

Over the next few weeks, Liam saw remarkable changes. Deals that had been on hold suddenly moved forward. New opportunities emerged out of nowhere. Even his personal life improved—his relationships became more meaningful, and he found time to mentor a few young entrepreneurs in the complex.

One evening, Liam stood on the rooftop garden of Everywhere Park, gazing at the city skyline. He reflected on how much had changed in such a short time. It wasn't just about business or financial success; it was about alignment. By organizing his life and focusing on God's promises, he had positioned himself for acceleration.

As he watched the sun dip below the horizon, Liam whispered a prayer of gratitude. He knew there was still much to do, but he was ready. With God, he could accomplish in days what others might take years to achieve. The season of acceleration had only just begun.

Reflection Points:

1. **Declutter Your Mind and Life**: Liam's story emphasizes the importance of

eliminating distractions and staying focused. What areas of your life need decluttering?

2. **Stay in Faith**: Like Liam, remind yourself of God's promises. Are you expecting God to move in your situation?

3. **Take Action**: Acceleration requires both organizing and action. What practical steps can you take today to position yourself for a breakthrough?

4. **30-Day Mission**: Consider going on a 30-day mission to organize your life and focus on your goals. Watch how much progress you can make in a short time!

15 | ACCELERATION

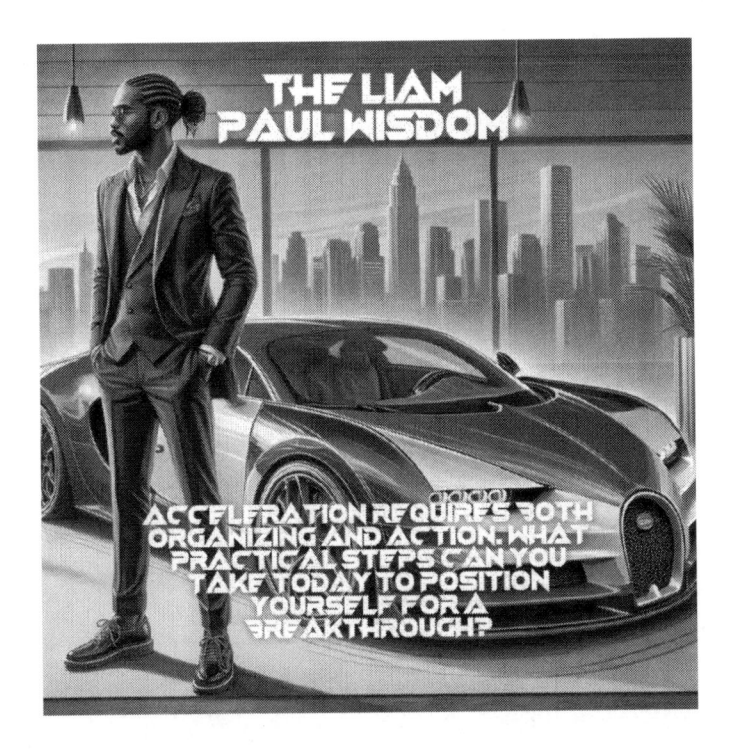

THE LIAM PAUL WISDOM

Acceleration requires both organizing and action. What practical steps can you take today to position yourself for a breakthrough?

Chapter Three: If You're Feeling Like Things Are Taking Too Long

If you're feeling like things are taking too long and going too slow, it's most likely the enemy.

Paul knew it was the enemy hindering him. He didn't say it was God closing a door, even though sometimes God does that.

1 Thessalonians 2:18 (NIV) *For we wanted to come to you—certainly I, Paul, did, again and again—but* **Satan blocked our way.**

New Living Translation *We wanted very much to come to you, and I, Paul, tried again and again, but* **Satan prevented us.**

English Standard Version *Because we wanted to come to you—I, Paul, again and again—but* **Satan hindered us.**

You need discernment so you will know when God is preventing you and when the devil is.

Romans 15:22 *That is* **why I have often been hindered** *from coming to you.*

2 Corinthians 11:14 *And no wonder, for* **Satan himself masquerades** *as an angel of light.*

Acts 16:6-7 *After* **the Holy Spirit had prevented them** *from speaking the word in the*

17 | ACCELERATION

province of Asia, they traveled through the region of Phrygia and Galatia. And when they came to the border of Mysia, they tried to enter Bithynia, but the Spirit of Jesus would not permit them.

2 Corinthians 12:7 *Or because of these surpassingly great revelations. So to keep me from being exalted above measure, I was given a thorn in my flesh,* **<u>a messenger of Satan, to torment me.</u>**

Once you discern that Satan is blocking you, you need to get intense with your prayer and authority. Ask God for wisdom and see which way to go. He can show you a reroute that is even quicker. Satan has held up things, but he has to let them go. You have to be strategic.

It's your time to receive, so don't allow Satan to rob you and your family another day. Kick him out of your home, your finances, your body, your goals, your church, your business, and your marriage! If Satan closed the door, then kick it down! Stop blaming every closed door on God. Sometimes God will prevent you from doing certain things, but this is why discernment is important. When Satan does it, don't put up with it, resist him and go get your stuff!

Find the Scriptures that fit your situation and put a beating on the Devil by quoting those verses back to him in full confidence. Jesus did this in Luke 4. It reads:

Luke 4:1 **Jesus, full of the Holy Spirit,** left the Jordan and was led by the Spirit into the wilderness, ² where for forty days he was tempted[a] by the devil. He ate nothing during those days, and at the end of them he was hungry. *³ The devil said to him, "If you are the Son of God, tell this stone to become bread." ⁴ Jesus answered, "It is written:* 'Man shall not live on bread alone.

Notice Jesus was full of the Holy Ghost and He used the Word of God to combat the enemy. You must do the same thing. You must be full of the Holy Ghost so you can discern when it's the devil. Watch how things will speed up when you start taking authority against the wicked one. **You've been in certain situations too long.** It's time for you to get out of those situations. It's time for you to have everything God said you can have. If you are supposed to have it, then GO GET IT!!

Luke 10:19 (AMP) Listen carefully: I have given you authority [that you now possess] to tread on serpents and scorpions, and *[the ability to exercise authority] over all the power of the enemy (Satan); and nothing will [in any way] harm you.*

19 | ACCELERATION

1 Peter 5:8-9 Be *sober-minded and alert*. Your adversary the devil prowls around like a roaring lion, seeking someone to devour. / <u>Resist him, standing firm</u> in your faith…

God Speaks in Visions and Dreams

Daniel 2:19-23 *During the night, the mystery was revealed to Daniel in a vision, and he blessed the God of heaven and declared: "Blessed be the name of God forever and ever, for wisdom and power belong to Him. He changes the times and seasons; He removes kings and establishes them. He gives wisdom to the wise and knowledge to the discerning."*

One thing is to stop telling everyone about your goals, dreams, vision, assignment, and career moves. Put your head down and work. If not, you just might get thrown in a pit, and pits make people pitiful, and pitiful will make you not do anything while you have a pity party. You're spending too much time sharing your dream versus doing your dream. All of that energy can go to doing something. You don't need validation, acceptance of the dream, or the gooey feeling of *liking that people like it*.

Nehemiah 2:12 (NLT) *I slipped out during the night, taking only a few others with me. <u>I had not told anyone about the plans God had put in</u>*

<u>my heart</u> *for Jerusalem. We took no pack animals with us except the donkey I was riding.*

Genesis 37:5-10 (GNBUK) *One night Joseph had a dream, and* <u>**when he told his brothers about it, they hated him even more**</u>. *He said, "Listen to the dream I had."*

God speaks and reveals important instructions through visions and dreams, but we must be careful who we share the details with. It just may hinder progress. Why? People will take your information and pervert it, change it, act like the devil did with Adam and Eve and say, "God didn't really mean that."

Numbers 12:6 *He said, "Hear now My words: If there is a prophet among you, I, the LORD, will reveal Myself to him in a vision; I will speak to him in a dream."*

Acts 16:9-10 *During the night, Paul had a vision of a man of Macedonia standing and pleading with him, "Come over to Macedonia and help us." After Paul had seen the vision, we got ready at once to leave for Macedonia, concluding that God had called us to preach the gospel to them.*

Pay attention to those dreams and visions because God often speaks to His people in this manner. Don't allow the enemy to rob you of what you saw in the vision. Keep it close and

21 | ACCELERATION

dear to your heart. Don't share it with everyone.

It's time to receive

Everything you know you're supposed to have is loosed. Things have been taking too long. Take authority and be strategic, and let's speed this up.

How long is up to you. The reason is because it's already yours.

Joshua 18:3

New Living Translation *Then Joshua asked them, "How long are you going to wait before taking possession of the remaining land the LORD, the God of your ancestors, has given to you?"*

English Standard Version *So Joshua said to the people of Israel, "How long will you put off going in to take possession of the land, which the LORD, the God of your fathers, has given you?"*

Berean Standard Bible *So Joshua said to the Israelites, "How long will you put off entering and possessing the land that the LORD, the God of your fathers, has given you?"*

King James Bible *And Joshua said unto the children of Israel, How long are ye slack to go* *to possess the land, which the LORD God of your fathers hath given you.*

What will slackness produce?

Proverbs 10:4 *He becometh poor that dealeth with a slack hand: but the hand of the diligent maketh rich.*

A slack or slow hand will produce poverty. Procrastination keeps many people poor. A diligent hand makes you rich! What are you spending your time on? Who are you spending your time with? Pay close attention to both and evaluate how much time you're wasting with either or both. Don't be slack, be diligent.

Chapter Four: The Liam Paul Discernment

Liam Paul's day started with a gnawing feeling in his gut. He couldn't shake the thought that something was hindering his progress, something unseen yet palpable. As he sipped his coffee, he recalled the words of Paul in **1 Thessalonians 2:18**, *"For we wanted to come to you—certainly I, Paul, did, again and again—but Satan blocked our way."* Liam had read this scripture countless times, but today, it resonated differently. He sensed that the delays in his projects weren't coincidental; they were strategic blockades.

Determined not to let the enemy win, Liam got down on his knees. He prayed in faith, asking God for wisdom and discernment. As he prayed, he felt a peace settle over him, and a thought came to mind: *"Be strategic. Take action."*

After finishing his prayer, Liam grabbed his journal and wrote down three key steps:

1. **Discern the Source**: He needed clarity on whether the delays were from God redirecting him or from the enemy blocking him.

2. **Seek Wisdom**: If it was the enemy, he needed divine wisdom to find a way around the obstacles.

3. **Take Strategic Action**: He couldn't just sit and wait. He had to move forward, but with a plan.

With these steps in mind, Liam started his day. He had a crucial meeting with a potential partner for his real estate venture. This deal had been dragging on for months, with constant back-and-forth and inexplicable delays. Before heading into the meeting, Liam whispered a prayer, *"Lord, if this has been blocked by the enemy, give me the strategy to break through."*

The meeting began, and like before, there were complications. The partner hesitated, citing concerns that had never been raised before. Liam listened carefully, discerning whether this was a genuine concern or another tactic to stall. Suddenly, he remembered **Daniel 2:19-23**, where God revealed mysteries to Daniel. He silently prayed, *"Lord, reveal the hidden things here."*

In that moment, Liam felt prompted to ask a specific question about the partner's hesitation. To his surprise, the partner admitted that they were unsure about the timeline and needed reassurance. Liam, armed with clarity,

25 | ACCELERATION

presented a revised timeline and a strategic plan that addressed their concerns. The atmosphere shifted. By the end of the meeting, they agreed to move forward.

Walking out of the building, Liam felt a surge of gratitude. He knew this victory wasn't just about business—it was about trusting God, discerning the source of delays, and taking strategic action.

That evening, Liam reflected on the day's events. He thought about Joseph and how sharing his dreams too soon led to jealousy and betrayal. He realized he had been too open about his goals and plans. From now on, he would be more discreet, sharing only with those who truly needed to know.

He recalled **Nehemiah 2:12**, *"I slipped out during the night, taking only a few others with me. I had not told anyone about the plans God had put in my heart for Jerusalem."* Liam decided to adopt a similar approach. He would work quietly, strategically, and with discernment.

As he closed his journal, Liam wrote one final note: "It's time to receive. Everything I know I'm supposed to have is loosed. This has taken too long. I will take authority over my circumstances, remain diligent, and stay focused on the path God has set before me. No more distractions, no more delays."_

Liam felt a renewed sense of purpose as he prepared for the next phase of his mission. He knew there would be more obstacles ahead, but he also knew that with discernment, strategic action, and God's guidance, he could overcome anything that tried to hinder his progress. This was only the beginning of a new, accelerated season in his life.

The next day, Liam rose early, determined to continue on his journey with faith and focus. He understood that breakthroughs didn't happen by chance—they required partnership with God, intentional planning, and unwavering perseverance.

As he stepped out of his apartment, ready to face the world, Liam whispered a final prayer: *"Lord, I thank you that today will be another step toward the promise You've given me. Grant me wisdom, strength, and the ability to move forward with confidence. In Your name, I walk boldly into the future."*

The season of discernment and strategic action had truly begun, and Liam was ready to run the race set before him.

27 | ACCELERATION

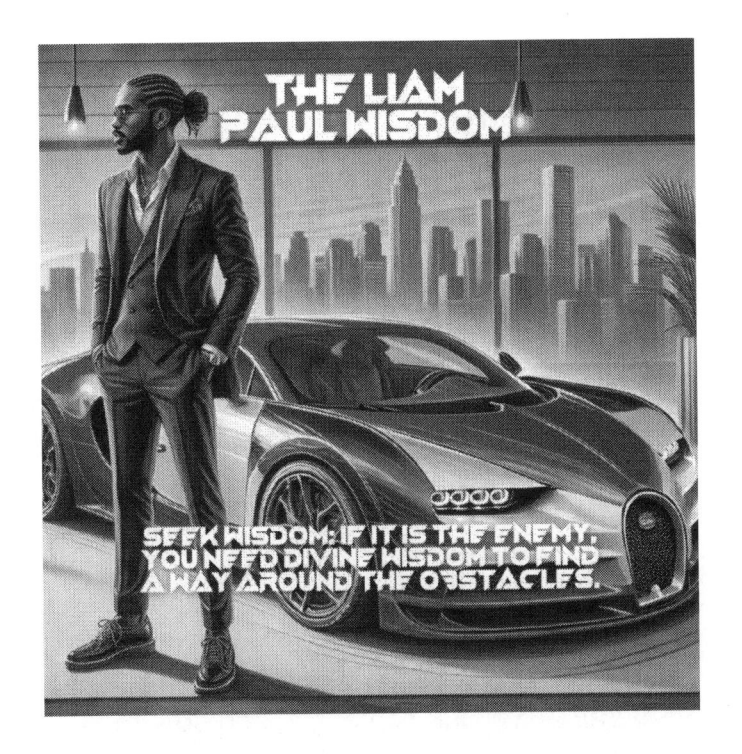

THE LIAM PAUL WISDOM

SEEK WISDOM: IF IT IS THE ENEMY, YOU NEED DIVINE WISDOM TO FIND A WAY AROUND THE OBSTACLES.

Chapter Five: Make *IT* So You Can Make It

Make Your Way

Joshua 1:8 *This book of the law shall not depart from your mouth, but you shall meditate on it day and night, so that you may be careful to do according to all that is written in it; for then you will make your way prosperous, and then you will have success.*

Making your way is about leveraging what you have to create what you need. It requires action and strategic use of available resources. Just as God told Joshua to meditate on His word day and night, confess it, and do it to make his own way prosperous, you too need to immerse yourself in God's way of doing things and take deliberate steps toward "MAKING YOUR WAY".

MAKE IT YOURSELF

2 Kings 6:1-5 *The company of the prophets said to Elisha, "Look, the place where we meet with you is too small for us.* **Let us go to the Jordan, where each of us can get a pole; and let us build a place there for us to meet***." And he said, "Go." Then one of them said, "Won't you please come with your servants?" "I will," Elisha replied. And he went with them. They went to the Jordan and began* *to cut down trees. As one of them was cutting down a tree, the iron axhead fell into the water. "Oh no, my lord!" he cried out. "It was borrowed!"*

In this story, you can see the company of prophets had a problem and they decided to MAKE what they needed themselves. They decided to build what they needed. They MADE something and that's why they succeeded in their endeavor. Many of you are trying to see how to make it in life. I'm encouraging you to use your resources to MAKE certain things so you can "make it in life". Stop waiting for others to provide for you. Provide for yourself by creating things with resources that are right in front of you.

In this story, cutting trees represents using accessible resources to build something new. The prophets didn't wait for ideal conditions; they went to the forest and started cutting down trees. Likewise, you need to identify the materials, tools, or information available to you and start building. Often, these resources are right in front of you, free for the taking.

Find and Leverage Resources

The "woods" symbolize apps, websites, or platforms like Google, ChatGPT, YouTube, Craigslist, Thumbtack, and more. You have access to a wealth of knowledge and tools that can help you make progress. Use them wisely.

Even if you don't own the tools you need, you can borrow them. In the passage, one prophet borrowed an axe to complete the task. Don't be afraid to seek help or leverage someone else's expertise or resources. Collaboration and borrowing are valid strategies when building your way to success.

Take Strategic Action

Just as the prophets acted by cutting wood and building, you must act on the vision God has given you. Whether it's gathering information, seeking mentorship, or using digital tools, take consistent, deliberate steps. Small actions, when compounded over time, lead to significant outcomes.

Remember: *"Make it so you can make it."* Your journey is a partnership between your effort and God's guidance. Stay diligent, keep learning, and trust that God will bless the work of your hands (Deut 28:12).

Reflection Questions:

1. What resources do you currently have that you can leverage?

2. Are there tools or information you need to borrow from others?

ACCELERATION

3. How can you take immediate action toward building your vision today?

Stay focused, stay disciplined, and watch how God accelerates your progress when you step out in faith.

Chapter Six: The Liam Paul Strategy

Liam Paul had always believed that success wasn't about waiting for perfect conditions—it was about using what was already in his hands. On a crisp morning at Everywhere Park, he sat on his balcony, reflecting on his current projects. Several ventures were in progress, but each felt like it was moving too slowly.

As he opened his Bible app, **Joshua 1:8** caught his attention: *"...for then you will make your way prosperous, and then you will have success."* The words struck a chord. Liam realized he had been waiting for external circumstances to improve before taking significant action. But the verse reminded him that he had the power to "make his way" by taking action with what he already had.

Inspired, Liam decided it was time to build. He listed out all the resources he had at his disposal—his network, digital tools, and the knowledge he had gained over the years. "The woods," he thought to himself, "are all around me. I just need to start cutting."

Later that day, he reached out to a mentor to borrow some equipment he needed for a new business idea. The mentor not only agreed to lend the equipment but also offered valuable advice. Liam smiled, remembering the story from **2 Kings 6**, where the prophets borrowed an axe to complete their task.

As he worked on his new project, Liam realized that he had been surrounded by resources all along—he just hadn't seen them clearly before. His digital tools, the people in his life, and even his past experiences were all part of the "woods" he could use to build something meaningful.

The next few weeks were transformative. By leveraging what he had and borrowing what he didn't, Liam made significant progress. He cut through delays, overcame obstacles, and built momentum. His venture, once stagnant, now had life and energy.

One evening, as he reflected on his journey, Liam wrote in his journal: *"It's not about waiting for perfect conditions. It's about using what you have and trusting God to guide the process. Make it so you can make it."*

With this newfound clarity, Liam knew he was ready for whatever came next. He had learned that success wasn't just about big breakthroughs—it was about small, consistent actions fueled by faith and determination. By building with what he had, he was well on his way to creating something extraordinary.

Reflection Points:

1. What untapped resources are available to you right now?

2. How can you leverage your network, tools, and knowledge to move forward?

3. Are there areas where you need to seek help or borrow resources?

THE LIAM PAUL WISDOM

"It's not about waiting for perfect conditions. It's about using what you have and trusting God to guide the process. Make it so you can make it."

Chapter Seven: The Power of Momentum

Momentum: the quantity of motion of a moving body, measured as a product of its mass and velocity.

Exodus 14:15 *Then the LORD said to Moses, "Why are you crying out to me? Tell the people to get moving!"*

You can't have momentum unless you're moving. Action produces momentum. God wants to accelerate us into His plan, but we must keep the motion going. We must keep moving forward.

Momentum is designed to get you to your destination. Once something is in motion, it keeps going unless there's friction.

Friction: *resistance, conflict, or animosity caused by a clash of wills, temperaments, or opinions.*

Friction is the force resisting the relative motion of solid surfaces. It is when there is a clash of wills. Too many opinions coming your way.

"You don't need an opinion when you have the truth on the matter."

Watch out for people and things that bring resistance to the will of God for your life. Get away from conflict, people's opinions, and all kinds of animosity. You're trying to go somewhere, but you keep rubbing up against things and people that cause friction. You have a solid plan from God but you're experiencing friction. Don't sabotage your dreams, assignments, and life's purpose just to please friction starters!

The early church had momentum, and they came across much friction, but they kept moving. The worst thing to do is stop when momentum is in motion.

You have to deal with friction. You must stop everyone who tries to stop the momentum.

Some of the friction is between you and you. You keep stopping yourself because of your overthinking. Many of you are resisting yourself. You're fighting within and it's causing friction. This is one big reason you're losing momentum and if you lose momentum, you will not accelerate.

Many of you want shortcuts to success, so you keep stopping the things that are challenging you. You think there is an easier and shorter way to get to the destination. But there are no shortcuts to success. **There is, however, a BETTER way to success, and it's God's path.** It's Spirit-led versus a carnal, worldly, American culture way.

37 | ACCELERATION

Acts 13:6-12 *They traveled through the whole island until they came to Paphos. There they met a Jewish sorcerer and false prophet named Bar-Jesus, who was an attendant of the proconsul, Sergius Paulus. The proconsul, an intelligent man, sent for Barnabas and Saul because he wanted to hear the word of God. But Elymas the sorcerer (for that is what his name means) opposed them and tried to turn the proconsul from the faith. Then Saul, who was also **called Paul, filled with the Holy Spirit, looked straight at Elymas and said, "You are a child of the devil and an enemy of everything that is right! You are full of all kinds of deceit and trickery. Will you never stop perverting the right ways of the Lord? Now the hand of the Lord is against you. You are going to be blind for a time,** not even able to see the light of the sun." Immediately mist and darkness came over him, and he groped about, seeking someone to lead him by the hand. When the proconsul saw what had happened, he believed, for he was amazed at the teaching about the Lord.*

Don't be afraid to confront people who cause friction. As you can see, Paul dealt with Elymas. You too must deal with people who try to pervert progress, cause friction, and hinder the ways of the Lord.

Also, don't be afraid to add to the momentum by including someone or something that will help keep it going.

Acts 11:22-26 *News of this reached the church in Jerusalem, and they sent Barnabas to Antioch. When he arrived and saw what the grace of God had done, he was glad and encouraged them all to remain true to the Lord with all their hearts. He was a good man, full of the Holy Spirit and faith, and a great number of people were brought to the Lord*<u>**. Then Barnabas went to Tarsus to look for Saul, and when he found him, he brought him to Antioch.**</u> *So for a whole year Barnabas and Saul met with the church and taught great numbers of people. The disciples were called Christians first at Antioch.*

Barnabas went and brought Saul back to help with the momentum at this new church plant. As a result, there was an acceleration in the spiritual growth at the church. Find people to work with who can help with the momentum and cause things to accelerate.

How to Keep the Momentum Going:

1. **Be clear about what you want.** If you're not, you're going to keep giving up on things that you should keep moving forward in.

2. **Don't make up excuses.** Keep the excuses out. Excuses keep you from moving. You will eventually give up if you keep making excuses.

3. **Don't be afraid to move faster than you're moving.** Sometimes your hesitation is simply doubt and fear. But when there is momentum, you need to pick up the pace, not slow down.

4. **Have a strong back.** When you have momentum, you need to have a strong back. Satan would love to stop what God is doing in your life. But you have to take on the responsibility to rebuke everything and everybody that tries to stop your momentum.

People are not going anywhere in life because they simply allow people and circumstances to stop the momentum. Fight back. Resist what's resisting you. Use your authority and keep the ball rolling.

5. **Stick with what's working.** Momentum stops when you're constantly switching things up. Momentum works with consistency.

Stay consistent, stay in faith, and watch God accelerate your progress!

Chapter Eight: The Liam Paul Momentum

Liam Paul had learned many lessons about building and taking action, but today's challenge was different—it was about keeping things moving. His latest venture, a social enterprise called "Everywhere Social" aimed at revitalizing the local community, was gaining traction. People were starting to take notice, and momentum was building.

As he sat in his office at Everywhere Park, reviewing plans for the next phase, Liam thought about **Exodus 14:15**: *"Why are you crying out to me? Tell the people to get moving!"* He knew that momentum wouldn't sustain itself—he needed to keep pushing forward.

With his team gathered around the conference table, Liam laid out the strategy for the next month. "We've made great progress, but we can't stop now. Momentum is on our side, and we need to keep moving forward. Let's be clear about our next steps and avoid unnecessary friction."

The team nodded in agreement. They knew what Liam meant by friction. In the past few weeks, they had faced resistance from a few local groups who didn't understand their

41 | ACCELERATION

mission. Yet, Liam had handled it well, confronting the issues directly without letting them derail their progress. He remembered **Acts 13:6-12**, when Paul confronted Elymas, the sorcerer who tried to hinder the work of God. "Sometimes," Liam had told his team, "you have to confront what's trying to stop you head-on."

Later that day, Liam met with a mentor who reminded him of the importance of adding positive forces to sustain momentum. Just like Barnabas had brought Paul to Antioch in **Acts 11:22-26**, Liam knew he needed to bring in more skilled individuals who could help keep things moving.

Inspired, he reached out to a few trusted colleagues and invited them to join the project. Each person brought something unique—skills, ideas, and energy that would keep the momentum alive.

That evening, as Liam reflected on the day's events, he wrote in his journal: *"Momentum is a gift, but it's also a responsibility. Keep moving, stay clear about your goals, confront friction, and surround yourself with the right people. That's how you sustain momentum."*

With renewed determination, he prayed, asking God for wisdom and strength to continue leading the project forward. He knew that as long as he stayed in motion, trusting God's guidance, nothing could stop the momentum from carrying him toward the vision God had placed in his heart.

Reflection Points:

1. Are there areas where you've allowed friction to stop your momentum?
2. How can you confront resistance without losing focus?
3. Who can you bring into your life or project to help sustain momentum?

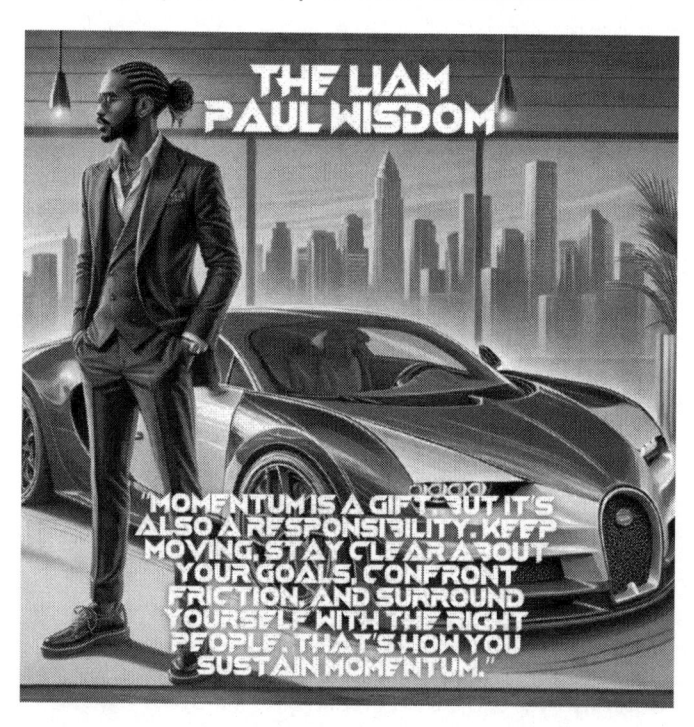

"MOMENTUM IS A GIFT, BUT IT'S ALSO A RESPONSIBILITY. KEEP MOVING, STAY CLEAR ABOUT YOUR GOALS, CONFRONT FRICTION, AND SURROUND YOURSELF WITH THE RIGHT PEOPLE. THAT'S HOW YOU SUSTAIN MOMENTUM."

Chapter Nine: Acceleration Will Happen When You Know THIS!

Knowledge is powerful, and one of the most critical things you need to know is this: *Everything you need is already here!* The resources, ideas, and opportunities you seek are not hidden in some far-off place. God placed everything on this earth for us to discover and use. When you truly understand this, it will accelerate things in your life. The key to unlocking this acceleration lies in finding what God has already provided.

When You Don't Know, You Suffer

Lack of knowledge is a direct cause of suffering. When you don't know what you have, you will live in lack. When you don't know how to access what belongs to you, frustration and stagnation take hold. Without the proper plan, strategy, and mindset, even the most abundant resources around you can seem useless.

Psalm 89:11 says, *"The heavens are thine, the earth also is thine: as for the world and the fulness thereof, thou hast founded them."*

God created the earth in such a way that it contains everything we would ever need. Gold, silver, oil, natural resources, copper, wood—it's all already here. Think about it: Cars, buildings, technology—they were all created using resources God placed on the earth from the beginning. Glass comes from sand. Paper comes from wood. Everything you see around you is made from materials that have always existed.

John 1:1-5 (KJV) *The same was in the beginning with God. All things were made by him; and without him was not any thing made that was made.*

God has already provided everything we need to live, prosper, and innovate. It's not about asking for new things; it's about uncovering what He has already given us. When you understand this truth, you unlock the ability to accelerate your progress.

Innovation from What's Already Here

Every invention, every major advancement in human history has come from using what was already here. God provided the resources, and He also gave us the creativity and intellect to use them.

Consider oil: God placed it in the earth, and He also provided the materials and intelligence needed to extract it and turn it into fuel. Think of the potential wealth if you owned land with oil:

Example Calculation: If an oil company extracts 100,000 barrels of oil worth $80 per barrel and your royalty rate is 20%, you would receive:

- **100,000 barrels × $80 = $8,000,000 total revenue**
- **$8,000,000 × 20% = $1,600,000 royalty to you**

This simplified example shows how God has already placed wealth in the earth, waiting for us to discover and use it. The same applies to countless other resources—gold, silver, wood, and even modern materials like steel and foam.

Psalm 104:24-25 *O LORD, how manifold are thy works! In wisdom hast thou made them all: the earth is full of thy riches.*

The Power to Get Wealth

Deuteronomy 8:18 tells us, *"You shall remember the LORD your God, for it is he who gives you power to get wealth, that he may confirm his covenant that he swore to your fathers, as it is this day."*

God not only placed resources on the earth, but He also gave us the ability to create, build, and innovate. He gave us the wit to design new things, the power to work, and the wisdom to strategize.

We are often praying for things that God has already provided. It's not hidden from us; it's hidden *for* us. Our job is to seek, discover, and utilize these resources. As **Isaiah 45:3** says, *"I will give you hidden treasures, riches stored in secret places, so that you may know that I am the LORD."*

Why Are We Poor?

If everything is already here, why do so many people still live in lack? The answer is simple: *We won't W.O.R.K.*

1. **Wit:** Christians often fail to use their wit—their God-given intelligence and creativity. **Proverbs 8:12** says, *"I wisdom dwell with prudence, and find out knowledge of witty inventions."* We have the mind of Christ, which gives us access to next-level ideas and solutions. When we don't operate in godly wit, we rob ourselves and the world of solutions.

2. **Occupy:** Many people won't occupy the spaces God has called them to. To occupy means to do business and take up residence where God has placed you. **Luke 19:13** says, *"Engage in*

business until I return." Instead of being preoccupied with distractions, we must focus on the business God has given us.

3. **Respond:** We fail to respond to God's call. There is a call to take back what the enemy has stolen and to make disciples of all nations. Yet, fear, laziness, and procrastination keep many from responding. **Proverbs 3:6** says, *"In all your ways acknowledge Him, and He will make straight your paths."*

4. **Keep at it:** Success requires perseverance. Many give up when things get tough. **2 Timothy 4:7** reminds us, *"I have fought the good fight, I have finished the race, I have kept the faith."* You must keep at it until you reach your goal.

Prosperity Is God's Idea

Prosperity is not greed; it's God's nature. Was God being greedy while creating the universe and all that it contains? No! Is HE poor? No! He created the world to reproduce, multiply, and sustain itself. This includes wealth, health, relationships, and everything necessary for life. Even the cycle of reproduction in humans, animals, and plants reflects God's design for prosperity.

1 Timothy 6:17 *Command those who are rich in this present world not to be arrogant nor to put their hope in wealth, which is so uncertain, but to put their hope in God, who richly provides us with everything for our enjoyment.*

God richly provides us with everything for our enjoyment. Yet, many in the church have rejected prosperity, believing it to be greed. This mindset has kept people in poverty and lack. But prosperity, in its true sense, is about having more than enough so you can be a blessing to others.

Final Thoughts

Everything you need to live, prosper, and fulfill your purpose is already here. God has given us resources, the ability to create, and the power to work. When you align with His plan, seek knowledge, and take action, acceleration will happen. Stop waiting for something new and start discovering what God has already placed around you.

Remember, God didn't create poverty—He created prosperity. It's time to rise up, work with what He has provided, and step into the abundance He designed for your life.

Chapter Ten: The Liam Paul Hidden Treasure

The early morning light filtered through the wide windows of Liam Paul's office, casting a golden glow on the neatly organized desk. He leaned back in his chair, sipping his coffee, and reflected on the conversation he had with his mentor the night before. "Everything you need is already here," his mentor had said. Those words struck a chord with Liam, igniting a sense of urgency and excitement within him.

Liam had always been a man of action, but lately, he had felt like something was missing. He was building, leading, and innovating, but progress had been slower than he expected. As he pondered those words, he realized that perhaps he had been looking in the wrong places—praying for new resources instead of fully utilizing what God had already placed around him.

With a newfound determination, Liam opened his laptop and began reviewing his current projects. He knew it was time to shift his mindset. He wasn't lacking resources; he was lacking perspective.

Discovering Hidden Potential

Liam's first task for the day was to meet with his real estate development team. They had been working on a new project to revitalize an old industrial area, but progress had stalled due to budget constraints. As the team gathered in the conference room, Liam addressed them with a fresh perspective.

"I've been thinking," Liam began, "we keep talking about what we don't have—funding, materials, approvals. But what if we focused on what we do have? God has already given us everything we need to succeed. It's just a matter of finding it."

The team exchanged curious glances. One of the project managers, Carla, spoke up. "That's great in theory, but practically speaking, we still need money to move forward."

"True," Liam agreed, "but let's break it down. What materials can we source locally at a lower cost? Are there any unused assets or properties we can leverage? And what about partnerships? We've been waiting for investors to come to us, but maybe we need to go out and seek them strategically."

The room grew silent as everyone considered Liam's words. Carla nodded slowly. "I know a local supplier who might be willing to provide materials at a discount if we offer them a stake in the project."

"Great!" Liam said with a smile. "Let's pursue that. And let's also map out every resource we currently have—land, equipment, relationships—and see how we can maximize them."

Hidden Treasures in Plain Sight

Later that afternoon, Liam took a walk around the industrial site. As he observed the abandoned buildings and overgrown lots, he remembered **Isaiah 45:3**: *"I will give you hidden treasures, riches stored in secret places, so that you may know that I am the LORD."* He realized that the potential of this area wasn't hidden from them—it was hidden *for* them. It was waiting to be unlocked by someone with the right perspective.

He spotted an old warehouse at the edge of the property. The structure was still sound, though the exterior looked worn and neglected. Liam made a mental note to explore the possibility of repurposing it instead of demolishing it.

As he continued walking, he noticed something else: the community around the site was vibrant, filled with small businesses and families. He hadn't fully considered the value of engaging the local community in the project. They weren't just building for profit; they were building to serve people. And those people could become partners in ways he hadn't imagined.

W.O.R.K.

That evening, Liam gathered his core team for a brainstorming session. He wrote four large letters on the whiteboard: W.O.R.K.

"Wit. Occupy. Respond. Keep at it," he said, underlining each word. "We've been praying for new opportunities, but what if we used our wit to come up with inventive solutions? What if we occupied this space fully, responding to the needs of the community and keeping at it until we see breakthrough?"

His business partner, James, leaned forward. "I like it. We've been so focused on what we don't have that we've ignored what's right in front of us. Let's start by making a list of potential partners in the community—local businesses, schools, and even non-profits. If we can engage them, we'll build something that benefits everyone."

"Exactly," Liam said. "God has already given us the resources and the people. Now it's up to us to W.O.R.K. and unlock the potential He's placed here."

The Shift in Mindset

Over the next few weeks, Liam and his team saw remarkable progress. By shifting their focus from what they lacked to what they had, they unlocked new opportunities. They secured a partnership with a local supplier, repurposed the old warehouse into a community center, and engaged local businesses in revitalizing the area.

One evening, as Liam stood on the rooftop of the newly renovated building, he reflected on how far they had come. He thought about **Deuteronomy 8:18**: *"You shall remember the LORD your God, for it is he who gives you power to get wealth."* Everything they needed had been there all along. They just had to see it and act on it.

Liam pulled out his journal and wrote: *"Acceleration happens when you realize that everything you need is already here. God has provided the resources, the people, and the ideas. It's up to us to discover them, use them, and keep moving forward."*

As he closed his journal, Liam felt a deep sense of gratitude. This journey had taught him that part of acceleration was about seeing the potential in what God had already provided and stepping out in faith.

Reflection Points:

1. Are there resources around you that you have overlooked?

2. How can you shift your mindset from scarcity to abundance?

3. What steps can you take today to fully occupy the space God has placed you in?

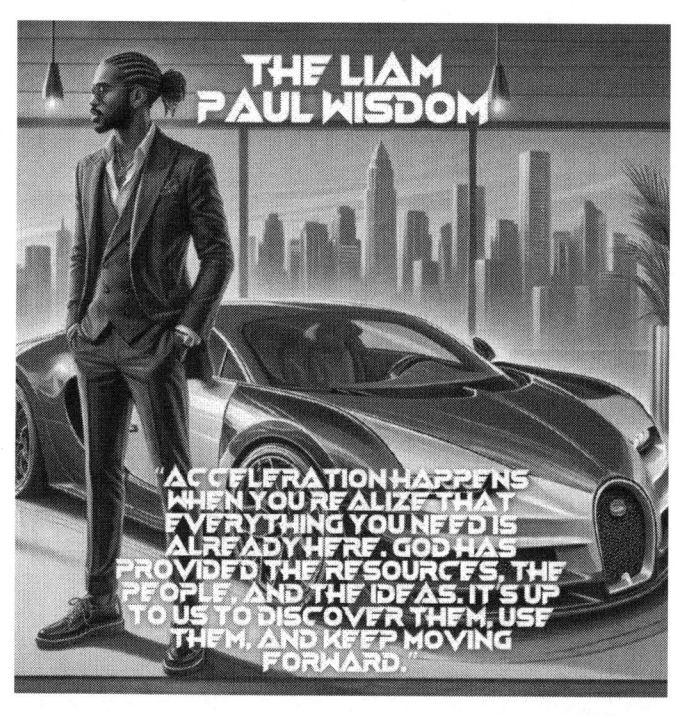

THE LIAM PAUL WISDOM

"ACCELERATION HAPPENS WHEN YOU REALIZE THAT EVERYTHING YOU NEED IS ALREADY HERE. GOD HAS PROVIDED THE RESOURCES, THE PEOPLE, AND THE IDEAS. IT'S UP TO US TO DISCOVER THEM, USE THEM, AND KEEP MOVING FORWARD."

Chapter Eleven: Everything Restored in a Day

Luke 8:43-48 *And a woman having an issue of blood twelve years, which had spent all her living upon physicians, neither could be healed of any, came behind him, and touched the border of his garment: and immediately her issue of blood stanched. And Jesus said, Who touched me? When all denied, Peter and they that were with him said, Master, the multitude throng thee and press thee, and sayest thou, Who touched me? And Jesus said, Somebody hath touched me: for I perceive that virtue is gone out of me. And when the woman saw that she was not hid, she came trembling, and falling down before him, she declared unto him before all the people for what cause she had touched him, and how she was healed immediately. And he said unto her, Daughter, be of good comfort: thy faith hath made thee whole; go in peace.*

This powerful story from Luke demonstrates how everything can change in a moment when faith meets divine power. The woman with the issue of blood had endured 12 years of pain, isolation, financial distress, and frustration. Yet, in one encounter with Jesus, her life was completely restored. What took over a decade of suffering and hopeless effort was reversed in a single day.

A Life of Isolation and Burden

According to Levitical law (Leviticus 15:19-30), a woman experiencing a blood discharge was considered ceremonially unclean. This meant she couldn't participate in religious rituals, social gatherings, or even touch others without making them unclean. For this woman, her condition wasn't temporary; it was chronic, lasting 12 long years. Imagine the weight of that burden—

- **Isolated**: She was likely shunned by her community and even her family. People avoided her to prevent becoming ceremonially unclean.

- **Financially Strained**: Scripture tells us she spent all her money on doctors, trying every remedy available. Despite her efforts, her condition only worsened.

- **Emotionally and Spiritually Burdened**: Beyond physical suffering, she bore the emotional toll of rejection and the spiritual pain of being cut off from worship, which was central to Jewish life.

This woman wasn't just dealing with a health issue; she was facing a compounded crisis.

Her physical ailment affected her finances, relationships, and self-esteem. Yet, what took 12 years of suffering was reversed in a single moment when she encountered Jesus.

God Restores One Area to Heal Many

One of the remarkable truths in this story is how God's restoration in one area of life can accelerate healing in other areas. The woman's act of faith not only brought physical healing but also paved the way for financial, social, emotional, and spiritual restoration.

Her Act of Faith

Despite the risk of public shame, she pressed through the crowd. She had a belief—a determined, unwavering faith—that if she could just touch the hem of Jesus' garment, she would be healed. In Jewish tradition, the hem of a garment symbolized a person's identity and authority. By touching His garment, she was symbolically acknowledging Jesus' authority over her condition.

Immediately, her bleeding stopped. Jesus, sensing that power had gone out from Him, asked who had touched Him. Trembling, she confessed, expecting rebuke. Instead, Jesus praised her faith and called her "Daughter," a term of acceptance and love. His words, "Go in peace," signified complete restoration—body, soul, and spirit. He was saying go and be prosperous in every area of life!

The Impact of Her Healing

1. **Physical Restoration**: The bleeding stopped immediately. After 12 years of constant suffering, her body was made whole.

2. **Social Reintegration**: Being healed meant she was no longer considered unclean. She could rejoin her community, touch others, and participate fully in social and religious life.

3. **Emotional Healing**: Jesus didn't just heal her body; He healed her heart. By calling her "Daughter," He affirmed her value and identity. This must have been a profound moment of emotional restoration after years of feeling like an outcast.

4. **Spiritual Renewal**: Her healing wasn't just physical; it was spiritual. She had acted in faith, and Jesus confirmed that her faith had made her whole. She could now worship freely and be part of the spiritual community again.

5. **Financial Restoration**: While the text doesn't explicitly state it, her financial restoration is implied. She had spent all her money on doctors with no results. Now, with her health restored, she could work, rebuild her life, and regain her financial stability.

Acceleration in a Day

This story is a testament to the power of divine acceleration. What took 12 years without Jesus was corrected in a moment with Him. This is what happens when God steps into a situation. The years of loss, frustration, and suffering are reversed in an instant.

When God moves, He doesn't just restore what was lost; He accelerates the process so that what took years to fall apart can be rebuilt in days. This is the essence of acceleration—divine intervention that speeds up the process beyond natural means.

By This Time Tomorrow

Just like the woman with the issue of blood, many of us have areas in our lives where we feel stuck, delayed, or broken. But when we encounter Jesus and act in faith, everything can change. What has taken years can be restored in a single moment.

The Principle of Faith

This story illustrates that faith requires action. The woman didn't wait for Jesus to come to her; she went to Him. Her faith wasn't passive—it was active, bold, and determined. She was literally breaking the religious law! Likewise, if we want to experience acceleration and restoration in our lives, we must be willing to act in faith and break religious rules!

- **Faith identifies the opportunity**: She recognized that Jesus was her opportunity for healing.

- **Faith takes action**: Despite the risks, she pressed through the crowd to touch Him.

- **Faith receives the result**: Her bold action led to immediate restoration.

A Word for You

Are there areas in your life that have been stuck for years? Have you been waiting, hoping, and praying for change? This story reminds us that one encounter with Jesus can change everything. Restoration and acceleration are possible when we act in faith.

God has the power to restore what was lost and accelerate your progress beyond what seems natural. Just as the woman experienced complete restoration in a single day, so can you. Step out in faith, press into His presence, and get ready for everything to be restored in your life.

By this time tomorrow, everything can change.

Chapter Twelve: The Liam Paul Restoration

The sun shone brightly over the city skyline as Liam Paul walked into his office at Everywhere Park. Today felt different. There was an air of anticipation, a stirring in his spirit that something significant was about to happen. He had just finished a morning devotional, reflecting on the story of the woman with the issue of blood and how her life had been restored in a single day through an act of faith.

Liam knew that restoration was possible for anyone who dared to believe. He had seen it happen in his own life, and today, he would witness it again—this time, for someone else.

A Desperate Call

As he settled into his chair, his phone buzzed. It was a call from a longtime friend, Marcus. Liam hadn't heard from him in years, and the tone in Marcus's voice immediately indicated that something was wrong.

"Liam, I need your help," Marcus began, his voice strained. "I've hit rock bottom. The business is failing, my family is falling apart, and I don't know what to do."

Liam listened intently, sensing the depth of his friend's despair. Marcus had been a successful entrepreneur once, but years of setbacks and poor decisions had left him broken, isolated, and financially drained—not unlike the woman with the issue of blood.

"Come to my office," Liam said firmly. "We'll talk, and we'll figure this out."

The Power of Perspective

An hour later, Marcus arrived, looking worn and defeated. As they sat across from each other, Marcus began to share his story—the failed ventures, the strained relationships, the mounting debt. Liam listened carefully, his mind racing through the principles he had been meditating on that morning.

"Marcus, I understand how overwhelming this must feel," Liam said after a pause. "But you need to realize something: everything you need for restoration is already here. You're looking at your circumstances as if they're permanent, but they're not. Just like the woman in the story who suffered for 12 years, everything can change in a moment when faith meets the right opportunity."

Marcus looked skeptical. "I don't know, Liam. I've tried everything. I've spent all my resources trying to fix things, and nothing has worked."

"That's because you've been trying to fix things on your own," Liam said. "But restoration doesn't come through striving alone; it comes through faith and strategic action. You need to stop focusing on what you don't have and start seeing what you do have."

An Act of Faith

Liam walked over to a whiteboard and wrote in bold letters: *Faith + Wisdom = Restoration*.

"Here's what we're going to do," he continued. "First, we're going to pray and trust God for wisdom. Then, we're going to list out every resource you still have—people, assets, skills. There's more in your hands than you realize. Finally, we'll come up with a strategy to rebuild, but this time, you'll be operating from a place of faith, not fear."

Marcus nodded slowly, something shifting in his demeanor. He was beginning to see a glimmer of hope.

Immediate Results

After their meeting, they got to work. Liam helped Marcus identify a few remaining assets he could leverage, including a property he had almost forgotten about and a connection with an old investor who might still be interested in his business. They drafted a proposal, made some calls, and by the end of the day, they had secured a meeting with the investor.

The next day, Marcus met with the investor, who agreed to fund a new venture. In less than 24 hours, what had seemed like an impossible situation began to turn around.

When Marcus called Liam with the news, his voice was filled with amazement. "Liam, I can't believe it. Everything is changing so fast. It feels like a miracle."

"That's because it is," Liam said with a smile. "When you step out in faith and be wise in your decision making, God accelerates the process. What took years to fall apart can be restored in a day when you partner with Him."

A Word of Encouragement

As Liam hung up the phone, he reflected on the power of faith and restoration. Just like the woman who had suffered for 12 years and was healed in a moment, Marcus had experienced a sudden turnaround because he dared to believe and take action.

Restoration isn't just about fixing what was broken; it's about accelerating into a new season of wholeness and prosperity. When we act in faith, God steps in and moves in ways that defy logic.

Liam knew that this was just the beginning for Marcus. And he also knew that there were many others out there who needed to hear this message—that everything they needed for restoration was already within reach. They just needed to act in faith.

With that thought, Liam began planning a Kingdompreneur seminar, confident that more lives would be changed. Because when faith meets wisdom, *everything can be restored in a day*.

Reflection Points:

1. Are there areas in your life where you feel stuck or delayed?

2. What resources do you currently have that you may have overlooked?

3. How can you step out in faith and take bold action toward restoration?

Remember, when you act in faith, God accelerates the process. What has taken years can be restored in a single day. By this time tomorrow, everything can change.

Chapter Thirteen: Accelerated Miracles and Business in a Day!

2 Kings 4:1-7 *The wife of a man from the company of the prophets cried out to Elisha, "Your servant my husband is dead, and you know that he revered the Lord. But now his creditor is coming to take my two boys as his slaves." Elisha replied to her, "How can I help you? Tell me, what do you have in your house?" "Your servant has nothing there at all," she said, "except a small jar of olive oil." Elisha said, "Go around and ask all your neighbors for empty jars. Don't ask for just a few. Then go inside and shut the door behind you and your sons. Pour oil into all the jars, and as each is filled, put it to one side." She left him and shut the door behind her and her sons. They brought the jars to her and she kept pouring. When all the jars were full, she said to her son, "Bring me another one." But he replied, "There is not a jar left." Then the oil stopped flowing. She went and told the man of God, and he said, "Go, sell the oil and pay your debts. You and your sons can live on what is left."*

This story highlights God's ability to bring about accelerated miracles. The widow's situation was desperate—she had lost her husband, and now creditors were coming to take her two sons as slaves to settle the family's debt.

According to the customs and legal framework of ancient Israel, creditors could act swiftly and harshly, especially when the debtor had no other assets to offer.

The widow needed an urgent solution, not just a temporary fix. She needed divine intervention that would change her financial situation permanently. And that's exactly what God did. He provided her with wisdom and a specific business idea that transformed her life—in a single day.

Immediate Threats and Swift Solutions

In ancient Israel, debt slavery was a common practice. If someone couldn't repay a loan, creditors had the legal right to take the debtor or their family members as bondservants. Although the Law of Moses provided some safeguards, such as releasing servants after six years (Exodus 21:2-4), creditors often acted swiftly when there were no assets to collect.

This widow was vulnerable—she had no income, no husband, and her sons were about to be taken. In this moment of crisis, she turned to the prophet Elisha, who represented God's voice in her life.

Notice Elisha's response: He didn't tell her to pray, fast for 30 days, or wait for a miracle to fall from the sky. Instead, he asked her a critical question: *"What do you have in your house?"* This question shifted her focus from what she lacked to what she already possessed. Her answer? *"A small jar of olive oil."*

Wisdom That Transcends Time

Elisha gave her clear, specific instructions:

1. **Borrow empty jars from neighbors**—a bold act of faith.

2. **Shut the door and pour the oil**—a private act of obedience.

3. **Sell the oil, pay the debt, and live on the rest**—a practical business plan.

The miracle didn't happen until she acted on the word. The oil kept flowing as long as there were empty jars. When the jars ran out, the oil stopped. This teaches us that God's provision is limitless, but it flows in proportion to our capacity to receive and act.

In one day, her life changed. She went from being a desperate widow on the verge of losing her sons to becoming a successful businesswoman with enough to pay her debts and live off the surplus.

Modern-Day Application

This story is not just about ancient times; it's a blueprint for modern believers facing financial challenges. When you are in a tight spot, instead of focusing on what you don't have, ask yourself: *"What do I have in my house?"*

God can use what you already have to bring about your breakthrough. It might be a skill, a resource, or an idea. The key is to act in faith and follow the wisdom He provides, often through spiritual leaders, mentors, or direct divine inspiration.

Deuteronomy 28:12 says, *"The Lord will open the heavens, the storehouse of his bounty, to send rain on your land in season and to bless all the work of your hands. You will lend to many nations but will borrow from none."* Notice that God blesses *the work of your hands*. The miracle happens when you start working with what you have.

Business Miracles in a Day

Elisha didn't tell the widow to diversify into ten different ventures or go to university to get a business degree. He gave her one clear instruction: *Start an oil business.* Often, we overcomplicate things by chasing too many ideas and unnecessary education. But acceleration happens when you focus on the one thing God has called you to do and do it well.

This principle is echoed in the New Testament. When Jesus needed to pay taxes, He didn't tell Peter to pray about it or find a new trade. Instead, He told Peter to go fishing—something Peter already knew how to do. *"Go to the lake and throw out your line. Take the first fish you catch; open its mouth, and you will find a four-drachma coin. Take it and give it to them for my tax and yours"* (Matthew 17:27).

Both the widow and Peter experienced accelerated miracles because they acted in faith and used what they had. God gave them specific instructions, and when they obeyed, provision came quickly.

The Role of Obedience

Obedience to God's specific instructions is a key factor in experiencing accelerated miracles. The widow didn't delay; she immediately gathered the jars and began pouring the oil. Likewise, Peter didn't hesitate; he went straight to the lake and caught the fish.

When God gives you a word—whether through scripture, prayer, or a trusted spiritual leader—act on it quickly. Delayed obedience can delay your miracle. As Elisha told the widow, *"Go, sell the oil and pay your debts. You and your sons can live on what is left"* (2 Kings 4:7). The same God who provided for the widow and Peter can provide for you.

A Call to Action

This is your season of acceleration. God is ready to move in your life, but He requires your participation. Stop waiting for ideal conditions and start working with what you have. Whether it's a skill, a resource, or an idea, put it to work and trust God to multiply it.

Remember, *"You will see the hands of God working in your life when He sees your hands working in your life."* The miracle is already in motion; it's time for you to step out in faith and do your part.

Focus on the one thing God has placed in your hands, obey His instructions, and watch as He accelerates your progress. Just as the widow's life changed in a day, so can yours. **This is your season. This is your moment. Get ready to see everything turn around in a day!**

Chapter Fourteen: The Liam Paul Miracle Business Solution

Liam Paul glanced at his phone, reading a message from one of his mentees, Jasmine. She was a single mother trying to build a small business, but she was overwhelmed by debt and the pressure to provide for her children. The desperation in her words hit Liam hard. He knew exactly what that kind of stress felt like. Without wasting any time, he invited her to his office at Everywhere Park for a meeting.

Jasmine arrived a short while later, visibly anxious. "Liam, I've tried everything," she said, her voice trembling. "I've taken out loans, worked extra hours, and even sold personal items, but it's never enough. Now, I'm at risk of losing my home. I don't know what else to do."

Liam listened intently, recalling the story of the widow in **2 Kings 4:1-7**, who was on the verge of losing her sons to creditors. Her situation had seemed hopeless, just like Jasmine's. But God had provided a solution through the prophet Elisha, who gave her specific instructions on how to start a business and pay off her debts.

"Jasmine, I know this feels impossible right now," Liam said gently. "But I believe there's a way out. Let me ask you something: What do you have in your house that you can use?"

Jasmine frowned. "I don't have anything of value. Just a few basic supplies and..." she paused, thinking. "Actually, I do have a small stock of handmade skincare products I've been working on as a hobby. But that's not enough to solve my problems."

Liam smiled. "That's exactly what you need. Sometimes, the solution is already in our hands; we just don't see it. Let's work with what you have."

A Bold Plan

Liam pulled out a notepad and began sketching a simple business plan. "Here's what we're going to do. First, we'll create a small batch of your products using what you already have. Then, we'll reach out to people in your network and offer them samples. Once they see how good your products are, we'll start taking orders."

"But what about the debt?" Jasmine asked, still skeptical.

"We'll use the initial sales to pay down some of it," Liam replied. "And once you gain momentum, you can scale up. The key is to act quickly and trust the process. Remember, the widow in the Bible didn't wait around for a miracle—she followed Elisha's instructions immediately. And God multiplied her efforts."

Encouraged by Liam's confidence, Jasmine agreed. Together, they spent the next few hours organizing her supplies and planning the first sales push.

The Miracle of Action

By the end of the day, Jasmine had produced a batch of skincare products and reached out to several friends and acquaintances. To her surprise, the response was overwhelmingly positive. People loved the idea of supporting her and were eager to try her products.

Within 24 hours, Jasmine had sold enough to cover a significant portion of her debt. More importantly, she now had a viable business with the potential to grow.

When she called Liam to share the good news, she could hardly contain her excitement. "Liam, it's happening! I didn't think it was possible, but things are turning around so quickly."

Liam smiled, grateful to see how God had accelerated Jasmine's progress. "That's the power of the simple business model," he said. "When you trust God and work with what you have, He multiplies your efforts. Just like the widow's oil, your business is going to keep flowing as long as you keep pouring."

A Lesson in Obedience

Jasmine's story was a modern-day reflection of the widow's miracle. She didn't wait for perfect conditions or a guaranteed outcome—she acted in faith, using what she had. And because she obeyed quickly, she experienced immediate results.

Liam knew that many people, like Jasmine, were sitting on untapped potential. They were waiting for something external to change, when in reality, the solution was already within their reach. It reminded him of **Deuteronomy 28:12**: *"The Lord will open the heavens, the storehouse of his bounty, to send rain on your land in season and to bless all the work of your hands."*

God blesses the work of your hands, not your intentions or idle prayers. Faith without works is dead, and miracles often require action.

An Ongoing Mission

After Jasmine's breakthrough, Liam felt inspired to help more people discover their potential. He decided to host a webinar titled "Business in a Day: How to Activate Your

Miracle." The goal was simple: to teach people how to identify their God-given resources, act in faith, and trust God for acceleration.

The webinar was a huge success. Dozens of attendees left with practical strategies and renewed hope. Many of them, like Jasmine, began seeing immediate results as they put their faith into action.

Reflection Points:

1. What do you have in your house that God can use?

2. Are you waiting for perfect conditions, or are you ready to act in faith?

3. How can you follow God's specific instructions in your current situation?

God can take what seems insignificant and turn it into more than enough. Just as the widow's life changed in a day, so can yours. **This is your season of acceleration—get ready for your miracle!**

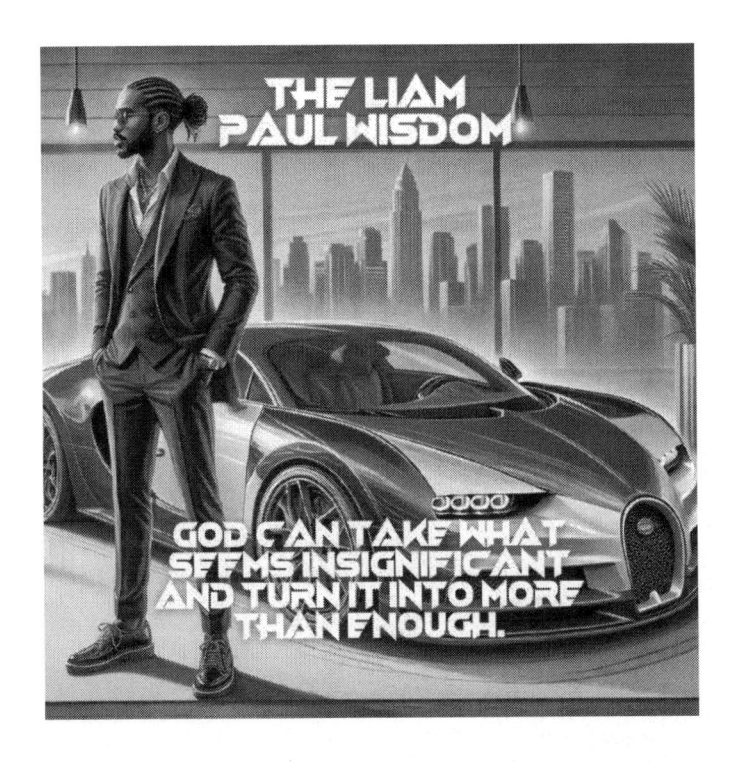

ACCELERATION

THE LIAM PAUL WISDOM

GOD CAN TAKE WHAT SEEMS INSIGNIFICANT AND TURN IT INTO MORE THAN ENOUGH.

Chapter Fifteen: Precision, Shifts, and Passive Income

Each day is a step, like climbing a 30-step ladder. Success isn't achieved in one leap—it's built step by step, one day at a time. What did you accomplish today that brings you closer to your goals? Each day's effort is a success that compounds into greater success. Take today as a step toward the top.

But here's the key: You must identify your "top." Without clarity about your ultimate goal, you'll wander aimlessly. Once you know your destination, take precise, disciplined steps toward it. Picture an arrow—you only have one shot each day, so aim carefully. Precision isn't just an asset; it's essential to success.

Precision is the Key to Success

David understood precision. When he faced Goliath, he wasn't distracted by the giant's size or strength. He focused on one target and used one rock. David's precision brought victory in a single battle.

1 Samuel 17:48-51 describes it vividly:

_"As the Philistine moved closer to attack him, David ran quickly toward the battle line to meet him. Reaching into his bag and taking out a

ACCELERATION

stone, he slung it and struck the Philistine on the forehead. The stone sank into his forehead, and he fell facedown on the ground. So David triumphed over the Philistine with a sling and a stone; without a sword in his hand he struck down the Philistine and killed him."

David's precision not only saved Israel but also transformed his own life. His reward was substantial:

1 Samuel 17:25-27: *"The king will give great wealth to the man who kills him. He will also give him his daughter in marriage and will exempt his family from taxes in Israel."*

David's willingness to embrace a new challenge brought influence and affluence. His tradition had been lions and bears, but stepping into a new battle—a 9-foot champion—accelerated his destiny.

Shifting for New Opportunities

When was the last time you did something for the first time? David's lions and bears didn't make him wealthy, but they prepared him for a new challenge. Sometimes, you need to shift your thinking and embrace a different lane within your industry or even step into a new one entirely.

You might be:

- An author writing the wrong type of books.

- An actor suited for sitcoms instead of movies.

- A singer meant for studio recordings instead of live tours.

- A teacher designed for high school rather than elementary.

- A real estate investor who hasn't tapped into multifamily properties.

The key is to recognize the new opportunity and shift. When David shifted to face Goliath, he didn't change who he was; he adapted his skills to a new challenge. His reward wasn't just financial—he gained influence, purpose, and the ability to help an entire nation.

The Shift in the New Economy

Today's economy is shifting. Many of the world's most valuable companies thrive not because of what they own, but because of what they control:

- **Facebook** creates no content but is worth $838 billion.

- **Uber** owns no taxis but is worth $100 billion.

- **Amazon** produces few products but is worth $1.5 trillion.

- **Airbnb** owns no properties but is worth $38 billion.

These companies leverage existing systems and resources, creating massive value without traditional ownership. In the same way, you may be in the right industry but need to shift your approach. For example, if you're in real estate, should you explore leveraging Airbnb?

Passive Income: The Game-Changer

As I always say, *"Don't trade time for money; invest money for time."* Passive income is the way to achieve that. It allows you to earn without constant effort, freeing up your time to focus on higher priorities and long-term goals.

Here are **seven examples** of passive income opportunities:

1. **Real Estate Investments**: Buy properties to rent out or operate as Airbnb rentals. These provide consistent cash flow and long-term appreciation.

2. **Dividend Stocks**: Invest in dividend-paying companies. As these companies grow, you'll receive regular payments without lifting a finger.

3. **Royalties**: Create intellectual property, such as books, music, or online courses, and earn royalties each time they're purchased or used.

4. **Peer-to-Peer Lending**: Lend money to individuals or businesses through platforms like LendingClub, earning interest on the loans.

5. **Digital Products**: Develop e-books, templates, or apps that can be sold repeatedly with minimal ongoing effort.

6. **Index Funds and ETFs**: Invest in low-maintenance funds that track market performance, providing steady, long-term returns.

7. **Business Ownership with Automation**: Create or invest in businesses that run with automated systems, such as e-commerce stores with drop-shipping models.

Every day is an opportunity to climb another step toward your goals. Identify your target, aim with precision, and be willing to shift when necessary. Whether it's embracing a new challenge like David or exploring passive income opportunities, success requires faith, discipline, and action.

85 | ACCELERATION

Take today as your step. What will you do differently? What shift will you embrace? Remember, God blesses the work of your hands. When you move in faith and precision, acceleration is inevitable.

Chapter Sixteen: The Liam Paul Precision

Liam Paul sat in the corner office of Everywhere Park, staring at a whiteboard filled with ambitious goals. Despite his company's success, something wasn't clicking. Growth had plateaued, and Liam knew it was time for a shift. He had been reflecting on the story of David and Goliath, particularly the lesson of precision and purpose. It was time to zero in on what mattered most.

Recognizing the Need for Change

Liam's phone buzzed. It was Sarah, a longtime friend and business consultant. "Liam," she said, "I've been analyzing your operations. You're doing great, but I think there's a better way. Have you considered leveraging Airbnb for some of your real estate holdings?"

Liam frowned. "Airbnb? I've always focused on long-term leases. That's been my bread and butter."

"Exactly," Sarah replied. "But the market is shifting. Short-term rentals are booming, especially in urban areas like the ones you're invested in. You don't need to overhaul your business—just shift your approach."

Embracing the Shift

Intrigued, Liam dove into research. The numbers were compelling. By converting just a portion of his properties into short-term rentals, he could significantly increase revenue. But it wasn't just about the money. This shift aligned with his broader vision: providing flexible, high-quality housing solutions that served a diverse range of clients.

He called an emergency meeting with his team. "We're making a change," he announced. "Starting today, we're testing the Airbnb model on three properties. If it works, we'll expand."

The team was hesitant but trusted Liam's leadership. Within weeks, the results were undeniable. The Airbnb properties were generating three times the income of traditional leases. More importantly, they were attracting a new customer base, expanding the company's reach.

Precision in Action

One evening, as Liam reviewed the numbers, he thought about David. Just as David had defeated Goliath with one precise stone, Liam had tackled his business challenges with a focused, strategic shift. He didn't abandon his expertise; he adapted it to a new opportunity.

Reflecting on the lesson of precision, Liam decided to apply the same principle to his personal life. He streamlined his daily routine, cutting out distractions and focusing on what truly mattered—faith, family, and purpose. The results were transformative. His business thrived, his relationships deepened, and his sense of purpose grew stronger.

The Passive Income Revelation

Encouraged by his success with Airbnb, Liam began exploring other passive income opportunities. He invested in dividend stocks, created a digital course on real estate investing, and even launched a peer-to-peer lending initiative. Each new venture was another step up the ladder of success, bringing him closer to his ultimate goal: financial and time freedom and the ability to give generously.

Liam often shared his journey with others, emphasizing the importance of precision and adaptability. "Success isn't about doing everything," he would say. "It's about doing the right thing at the right time with precision. And when you're willing to shift, God accelerates your progress."

89 | ACCELERATION

Liam's story is a reminder that success requires both precision and the willingness to adapt. Whether it's shifting your business strategy, embracing a new opportunity, or creating passive income streams, the key is to take focused, disciplined action.

What shift do you need to make today? What step will you take toward your goal? Remember, God blesses the work of your hands. When you move in faith and precision, acceleration is inevitable. **Start stepping up. This is your season!**

Chapter Seventeen: The Liam Paul Mastery

Teaching the Principles

As news of Liam's success spread, people began reaching out, eager to learn how he had turned a stalled project into a thriving community hub. Recognizing an opportunity to share the lessons he had learned, Liam decided to host seminars and webinars on acceleration.

At his first seminar, held in the renovated community center, the room was packed with entrepreneurs, community leaders, and dreamers. Standing confidently at the front, Liam opened with a bold statement: "Acceleration happens when you realize that everything you need is already here. The key is to discover it, use it, and keep moving forward."

Over the next hour, he walked the audience through the principles of W.O.R.K. He explained how wit, occupying spaces fully, responding to opportunities, and perseverance were the pillars that had driven his success. He shared personal stories of setbacks, breakthroughs, and the power of shifting one's mindset from scarcity to abundance.

During the Q&A session, a young woman raised her hand. "How do you deal with fear of failure when stepping out?" she asked.

Liam smiled, "I walk by faith, and you can't let fear paralyze and rob you. Remind yourself of this: God has already placed what you need within your reach. When you focus on what you have instead of what you lack, fear loses its grip. I don't fear failure, I have faith in success."

The audience erupted into applause. Liam could see the excitement in their eyes—they were ready to take action.

Expanding the Mission

The success of the seminar led to the launch of a series of webinars that attracted participants from across the country. Liam's teachings resonated with people in various fields—business, ministry, education, and more. His straightforward approach, combined with his faith-based perspective, made the principles accessible and actionable.

One evening, after a particularly successful webinar, Liam reflected on how far he had come. He remembered the early days when things were moving slow and friction was all around. Now, he was helping others unlock their potential and accelerate their progress.

Pulling out his journal, he wrote: *"Teaching others is the next step in my journey. It's not enough to succeed—I must help others do the same. Together, we can create lasting impact."*

With that thought, Liam knew his mission had expanded. It was no longer just about building projects; it was about building people.

Bonus Chapter: The Anatomy of a Kingdom Business—Lessons from Liam Paul's Bugatti

A car is a masterpiece of engineering, with every component designed to work together to create motion, speed, and direction. Just like a car, a business is made up of various parts that must function in harmony to achieve success. For Kingdompreneurs, understanding these components can be the key to accelerating your business toward its God-given purpose. In this chapter, we'll explore the car's frame, engine, driver's side, wheels, and interior as analogies for essential business elements.

The Frame and Color: Your Branding

The frame and color of a car are the first things people see. They define its identity and set the tone for how it's perceived. Similarly, your business's branding—its name, logo, colors, and overall design—is your frame. It's the visual and emotional identity that tells your audience who you are and what you stand for. It's the language, the culture, the customer service. All these things create your brand identity. Make sure you're intentional about your culture.

- **Storytelling Through Branding:** As Donald Miller explains in *Building a*

Story Brand, your brand should communicate a clear and compelling promise to your customers. It's not just about looking good; it's about telling a story that resonates with your audience.

- **Consistency Matters:** The Bugatti's sleek, recognizable design reflects luxury and performance. Likewise, your brand must consistently deliver on its promises to build trust and loyalty.

Your branding frames your business and **sets expectations**, making it the foundation of everything else.

The Engine: Your Marketing

The engine is the heart of the car, converting fuel into motion. In a business, marketing is your engine. It's the system that takes your vision and converts it into action, creating momentum and driving sales.

- **Fueling Your Marketing Engine:** A well-designed marketing strategy, like a high-performance engine, requires the right fuel—clear messaging, targeted campaigns, and a deep understanding of your audience. As Miller emphasizes, make your customer the hero of your story. **Show them how your product solves their problem.**

- **Efficiency and Power:** The Bugatti's engine is engineered for maximum speed and efficiency. Similarly, your marketing efforts must be efficient, using data and tools like AI to reach the right people at the right time with the right message.

Marketing is what makes your business move. Without it, you might have a great product, but no one will know about it.

The Driver's Side: Your Leadership

No matter how powerful a car is, it's useless without a driver. The driver's side represents leadership—the guidance and decision-making that steer the business.

- **Visionary Leadership:** Great leaders know the destination and plot the best route to get there. Like the designers of Bugatti, who envisioned creating the fastest, most luxurious car, you need a clear vision for your business.

- **Decision-Making:** As the driver, you decide when to accelerate, slow down, or change direction. Good leadership involves making timely decisions that align with your purpose and goals.

- **Empowering the Team:** Leadership is not just about steering; it's also about inspiring and aligning your team to move in the same direction.

The driver's role is critical. Without leadership, the business has no direction and risks stalling.

The Wheels: Your Sales Efforts

The wheels are what connect the car to the road, transferring the engine's power into motion. In a business, sales efforts are the wheels that turn marketing into revenue.

- **Building Trust:** Sales, as Miller highlights, should focus on solving customer problems rather than pushing products. People buy from businesses they trust.

- **Clear Communication:** Your sales team should echo the clarity and simplicity of your marketing message. Confusion is the enemy of sales.

- **Traction and Momentum:** Just as wheels need good tires to grip the road, your sales team needs the right tools and training to gain traction and build momentum.

Sales efforts make the connection between your business and your customers, ensuring that the power generated by your marketing engine isn't wasted.

The Interior: Your Products and Services

The interior of a car represents the experience it offers to the driver and passengers. In business, this is your product or service—what customers experience when they engage with you.

- **Exceeding Expectations:** The Bugatti's interior is a masterpiece of craftsmanship, combining luxury with functionality. Your product or service should deliver exceptional quality and value that exceeds customer expectations.

- **Customer-Centric Design:** Just as the Bugatti's interior is designed with the user in mind, your offerings should be tailored to meet the specific needs and desires of your audience.

- **Continuous Improvement:** The best cars and products are constantly refined. Seek feedback and make improvements to stay ahead of the competition.

Your products and services are what your customers experience directly. They are the fulfillment of your brand's promise and the reason customers keep coming back.

The Kingdompreneur's Car in Motion

When all these components work together, the car—your business—moves forward with speed and efficiency. The frame (branding) sets the identity, the engine (marketing) provides power, the driver (leadership) steers, the wheels (sales) connect to the road, and the interior (products and services) ensures a satisfying journey.

Just like a Bugatti, your business is built for acceleration. By understanding and optimizing each component, you can achieve the kind of success that not only transforms your life but also impacts the Kingdom of God.

This is your season to get behind the wheel, turn on the engine, and press the accelerator. Let's go!

Doc Murphy

ACCELERATION

THE LIAM PAUL BUGATTI

JUST LIKE A BUGATTI, YOUR BUSINESS IS BUILT FOR ACCELERATION. BY UNDERSTANDING AND OPTIMIZING EACH COMPONENT, YOU CAN ACHIEVE THE KIND OF SUCCESS THAT NOT ONLY TRANSFORMS YOUR LIFE BUT ALSO IMPACTS THE KINGDOM OF GOD.

About the Author

Doc Murphy is a serial church planter and Kingdompreneur. He travels planting churches with his wife Mary around the USA. He is the Founder of The Everywhere Network (a church planting family)

He is also the founder of Creative Apostle Everywhere. CAE is a record label that produces all genres of Christian music. He is the author of several books and is an accomplished kingdompreneur, success coach, author, songwriter and music producer. For more information, log on to our website at www.docmurphy.net

Other Books and Products by Doc Murphy

Mature

J.O.Y.

Becoming The Balanced You

Building Permit

Breaking The Grip of Oppression

S.I. Supernatural Intelligence

Faith

Becoming The Balanced You

J.O.Y.

Frequency

Where is My Health

Special Ops Leadership

The Everywhere Magazine

The Laborers Are Plenty

Understanding and Discovering the Y in U

Born for This

The Conqueror's Mentality

Eagle Leaders

Five + One Series

Transition

YOU Success

Nonnegotionables

The God of Increase

Dream Responsibly

Kingdompreneur

#Everywhere

Small Church Large Church

Go Ready Set!

History Makers

The Apostolic Church

Full Time Believing

The Supernatural Church

King Album

Radical EP by Mariee Murphy

Transition Ep

DOCtrine Ep

Future Risk It? EP by Mariee Murphy

Order these products @ amazon.com

Order at www.docmurphy.net
YOU Success Book by **Doc Murphy**
$15
YOU SUCCESS
THE FORMULA TO HELP YOU
DOC MURPHY
Explore how to identify what success uniquely means for YOU!
Understand the Importance of Dreams and Visions
Learn how YOU can differentiate yourself from others and create your own path to success using God's wisdom.
AVAILABLE IN PAPERBACK, E-BOOK, AND AUDIOBOOK FORMATS.
Audio Book
Paperback
E-book

Made in the USA
Columbia, SC
08 February 2025